MEYER
GAZZOTTI
VEHLMANN

# CLEAR BLUE
# TOMORROWS

CINEBOOK
*EXPRESSO*

Original title: Des Lendemains sans Nuage

Original edition: © Editions du Lombard (Dargaud-Lombard s.a.) 2014
by Meyer, Gazzotti & Vehlmann
www.lelombard.com
All rights reserved

English translation: © 2015 Cinebook Ltd

Translator: Jerome Saincantin
Lettering and text layout: Design Amorandi
Printed in Spain by EGEDSA

This edition first published in Great Britain in 2016 by
Cinebook Ltd
56 Beech Avenue
Canterbury, Kent
CT4 7TA
www.cinebook.com

A CIP catalogue record for this book
is available from the British Library

ISBN 978-1-84918-284-3

F.G. WILSON ENSLAVED THE WORLD IN THE MOST INSIDIOUS WAY...

HE DIDN'T SEIZE POWER THROUGH A COUP. NOR WAS HE ELECTED. ACTUALLY, WILSON ISN'T EVEN A POLITICIAN.

HE'S A BUSINESSMAN.

AND WE FREELY AGREED TO BUY INTO THE TECHNOLOGICAL COMFORT HE OFFERED: BIOMECHANICAL PROSTHESES, SYNTHETIC ORGANS...

THE NEW ZX·350 .TECHNOLAB.

WILSON IS 115 YEARS OLD AND DOESN'T LOOK A DAY OVER 30. WHO'D REFUSE THAT KIND OF IMMORTALITY?

WHEN TECHNOLAB LAUNCHED THE CEREBRAL IMPLANT, A BIOCHIP THAT OPTIMISED PHYSICAL AND MENTAL ABILITIES, NO ONE WOULD HAVE DREAMED OF GOING WITHOUT IT. NOWADAYS, THEY'RE IMPLANTED AT BIRTH EVERYWHERE IN THE WORLD.

AND WHAT COULD BE MORE NATURAL THAN HAVING THIS IMPLANT INCLUDE A 'NEURONAL PROVISION' PROHIBITING ITS WEARER FROM 'HARMING F.G. WILSON'?...

THAT'S HOW DISSENT BECAME IMPOSSIBLE.

THAT'S HOW WE CREATED A TYRANT COMMENSURATE WITH OUR TIMES: IMMORTAL AND OMNIPOTENT.

EVEN SO, I'M GOING TO TRY AND CHANGE THE COURSE OF HISTORY.

MY NAME IS NOLAN SKA. I'M AN ENGINEER.

THROUGH MY CLANDESTINE RE-SEARCH, I'M GOING TO BE THE FIRST MAN TO TRAVEL BACK IN TIME.

I MUST FIND WILSON.

NOT TO KILL HIM. MY CEREBRAL IMPLANT WOULDN'T LET ME.

BUT I STUDIED TECHNOLAB'S ARCHIVES VERY CAREFULLY, AND I FOUND OUT THAT WILSON DIDN'T ALWAYS WANT TO BE A BUSINESSMAN.

HIS FIRST PASSION WAS WRITING. HE WAS GIFTED, AND HE COULD HAVE BECOME A FAMOUS AUTHOR IF AN UNFORESEEABLE INCIDENT HADN'T DERAILED THAT AMBITION.

ON MAY 12, AT THE CAFÉ DE PARIS, THE ONLY COPY OF WILSON'S FIRST NOVEL WAS STOLEN.

PENNILESS, DISHEARTENED BY THE THEFT, HE GAVE UP WRITING AND GOT A JOB AS AN ACCOUNTANT WITH THE YOUNG COMPANY TECHNOLAB BEFORE CLIMBING ALL THE WAY UP ITS RANKS.

IT'S NOT 'HARMING F.G. WILSON' IF I GIVE HIS LITERARY CAREER A LITTLE BOOST, IS IT?

MY... MY MANUSCRIPT!...

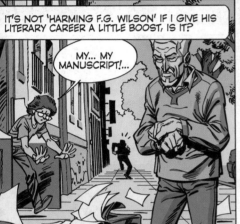

LET ME HELP YOU.

DON'T TOUCH THESE PAGES!

DAMMIT! YOU'VE GOT TO BE JOKING!

...Our hero then dashes to the door bfore opening it. He opens it and exclaimes bfore the evil Zarkor: 'You're goose is cooked Zarkor! I'm going to send you strait to hell!' Then Zarkor turns around and fires his laser at Silver, which Silver swiftly avoids by diving to the side before shooting back very quickly. Zarkors is hit and cries out: 'Curse you! You won't get away with this!', and shoots another laser bolt which ricochau

Page 3

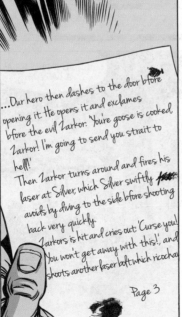

HOW COULD I HAVE BEEN NAIVE ENOUGH TO BELIEVE WILSON'S OFFICIAL BIOGRAPHY WHEN IT SPOKE OF 'LITERARY GENIUS'?...

SAY, MIND BUYING ME A DRINK?

I'M MEETING A BIG PUBLISHER TOMORROW. MY NOVEL'S GONNA BE A HIT!

THAT GUY CAN'T WRITE. HE'S GOING TO GET BLACKLISTED FOR GOOD, ACTUALLY!

IT'S ABOUT THIS GUY WHO'S GOT BIOMECHANICAL PROSTHESES THAT TURN HIM INTO A SUPERMAN.

UNLESS ...

I HEARD THAT PUBLISHERS ALWAYS REFUSE THE FIRST NOVELS THEY GET FROM SOMEONE.

WHAT?

IT'S A TRADITION TO TEST POTENTIAL AUTHORS. YOUR FIRST MANUSCRIPT WILL BE SACRIFICED. I HOPE YOU'RE NOT OVERLY ATTACHED TO IT!

ON THE OTHER HAND, YOU COULD ... OFFER THEM A SHORT STORY TO BEGIN WITH. I COULD GIVE YOU SOME ADVICE. I... I KNOW A BIT ABOUT WRITING.

I DON'T KNOW THE FIRST THING, BUT I HAVE NO CHOICE!

**IMPOSSIBLE!** WHAT COULD I WRITE ABOUT? I POURED EVERYTHING I HAD INTO MY MASTERPIECE: *SILVER VERSUS THE MORLOFFS!*

WELL, IT COULD TALK ABOUT ... WHAT THE FUTURE HOLDS FOR US... ER...

...I HAVE TO REMEMBER WHAT I READ IN TECHNOLAB'S ARCHIVES...

WHAT WAS THE NAME OF THAT PENAL METHOD INVENTED IN THE 2040S? THAT COULD BE A GOOD IDEA FOR A SHORT STORY...

THE '100% METHOD' – I REMEMBER NOW. WRITE THIS DOWN!

...YOU DON'T HAVE A LAPTOP?

NO WAY! I WRITE EVERYTHING BY HAND. I JUST DON'T GET COMPUTERS.

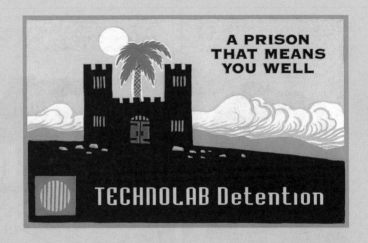

A PRISON
THAT MEANS
YOU WELL

TECHNOLAB Detention

The 100% method

— DAISY, PLEASE, LISTEN TO ME. I HAVE A CONFESSION TO MAKE... I... I LOVE YOU.
— WHAT WAS THAT?

— AAARGH, DAISY, DON'T MOCK ME. YOU HEARD ME VERY WELL! CIRCUMSTANCES ARE AGAINST ME, BUT I AM SINCERE.

— KEVIN! THAT'S MONSTROUS! JOHN, MY FIANCÉ, HAS JUST BEEN BURNED ALIVE IN AN ACCIDENT, AND YOU SPEAK TO ME OF LOVE?!...

— AARGH, DAISY, LOVELY DAISY, DON'T BE CRUEL. IF YOU DO NOT BELIEVE MY WORDS, THEN LOOK INTO MY EYES! THEY WILL TELL YOU I SPEAK THE TRUTH!

— OHH, KEVIN! COULD IT BE? AFTER ALL THOSE YEARS OF LYING, OF BETRAYING EVERYONE, COULD YOU TRULY HAVE FEELINGS FOR SOMEONE...?

♪ JOIN US TONIGHT FOR MORE OF *THE FLAMES OF LOVE!* ♪

ZOOM IN, PLEASE.

...DIRECTOR, NUMBER 1641 IS STILL RESISTING YOUR METHOD. HE WORRIES ME...

COME NOW, OTTO... YOU'RE EXAGGERATING AS USUAL!

ARE ALL THE SHRINKS AT TECHNOLAB DETENTION AS ALARMIST AS YOU?

ER... USUALLY, AFTER TWO MONTHS OF OUR TREATMENT, THE INMATES ARE COMPLETELY SUBDUED BY OUR 100% METHOD...

...WHEN THEIR IMPRISONMENT BEGINS, THEY HAVE NO INTEREST IN WATCHING *THE FLAMES OF LOVE*...

...HOWEVER, THEY PROGRESSIVELY BEGIN TO GET INVOLVED IN IT, SINCE WATCHING THAT SOAP IS THE ONLY AUTHORISED ACTIVITY — MANDATORY, I SHOULD SAY — IN OUR PENITENTIARY.

I KNOW ALL THAT, OTTO. I INVENTED THE 100% METHOD! WHAT ARE YOU DRIVING AT?

NUMBER 1641 HAS BEEN HERE FOR THREE MONTHS AND REMAINS UNRESPONSIVE TO OUR TREATMENT. A SITUATION WE'VE NEVER EN-COUNTERED UNTIL NOW!

HE WILL CRACK, MY DEAR OTTO. HE WILL CRACK, LIKE ALL THE OTHERS!

EXIT 3

TWEEEEET... OUTSIDE RECREATION... ALL INMATES TO THE COURTYARD.

9

'THE POINT OF A PRISON IS TO ESCAPE!' I KEEP TELLING MYSELF, OVER AND OVER AND OVER.

IF I HADN'T DONE SO FROM THE MOMENT I ARRIVED HERE, I'D HAVE BECOME LIKE ALL THE OTHER CONS: BRAIN DEAD!

'THE POINT OF A PRISON IS...'

HEY, 1641... 20 TO 1 THAT DAISY FALLS FOR KEVIN'S CHARM!

20 TO 1 THAT DAISY'S DIVORCED DOG WILL MARRY KEVIN'S CAT...

WOOF
WOOF
WUF          WOOF

?

IT'S KINDA SCARY, REALLY!

WHAT?! YOU CALLED DAISY A FAT COW?

I SURE DID!

HEY, 3624!

EVEN PITBULL, THE LEGENDARY TOUGH GUY, IS NOTHING MORE THAN A VEGETABLE STUPIDLY DREAMING OF BECOMING DAISY'S FIANCÉ.

SAY IT AGAIN!!

DAISY'S A FAT COW, FAT COW, FAT COW...

SNOK

TWEE    TWEEEEEEE

FIGHTING'S FORBIDDEN, PITBULL! IF YOU FORGET AGAIN, WE'LL TAKE AWAY YOUR SOAP WATCHING PRIVILEGES!!!

NO! NOT MY SOAP!

YEAH! WE'D RATHER YOU KEPT HITTING US!

TELL ME AGAIN HOW DAISY IS...

DON'T FORGET ABOUT HER CLUB FOOT THIS TIME!

?

?

GENTLEMEN, YOUR ATTENTION PLEASE. OUR OLDEST INMATE HAS JUST LEFT US...

HE WAS ONE OF THE VERY FIRST TO TAKE ADVANTAGE OF OUR METHOD. GOD REST HIS SOUL.

YOU CAN WATCH HIS FUNERAL LIVE AFTER THE BROADCAST OF TONIGHT'S *THE FLAMES OF LOVE*.

POOR GUY! TO DIE BEFORE THE SHOW ENDS!

YEAH! HE'LL NEVER KNOW IF KEVIN AND DAISY...!

IDIOTS! AS IF A SOAP LIKE THAT ONE COULD EVER END! AW, WHAT DO I CARE ANYWAY?! TOMORROW I'LL BE LONG GONE!

WARNING... END OF MEAL TIME.

EPISODE 23886 OF *THE FLAMES OF LOVE* STARTING IN SEVEN SECONDS... SIX... FIVE... FOUR... THREE...

OFFICER? THIS IS 1641. REQUESTING PERMISSION TO USE THE PRIVATE CORNER.

GRANTED, 1641!... MAKE IT QUICK!

THEY BURN THE HEART...

...OF THE LION AND THE DOVE...

...ONCE KINDLED, THEY NEVER GO OUT...

...IT'S *THE FLAMES OF LOOOOOVE!*

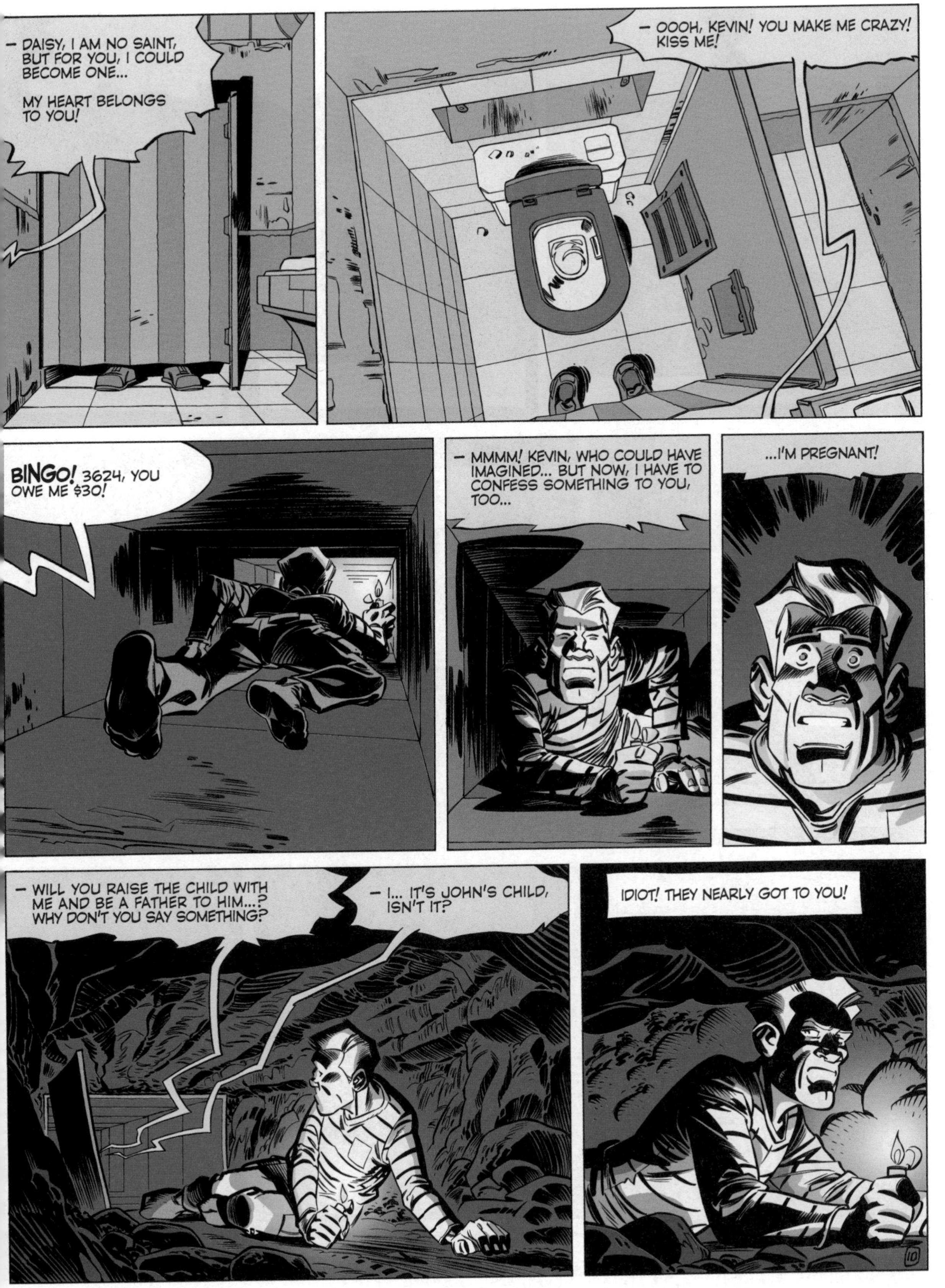
– DAISY, I AM NO SAINT, BUT FOR YOU, I COULD BECOME ONE...
MY HEART BELONGS TO YOU!
– OOOH, KEVIN! YOU MAKE ME CRAZY! KISS ME!
BINGO! 3624, YOU OWE ME $30!
– MMMM! KEVIN, WHO COULD HAVE IMAGINED... BUT NOW, I HAVE TO CONFESS SOMETHING TO YOU, TOO...
...I'M PREGNANT!
– WILL YOU RAISE THE CHILD WITH ME AND BE A FATHER TO HIM...? WHY DON'T YOU SAY SOMETHING?
– I... IT'S JOHN'S CHILD, ISN'T IT?
IDIOT! THEY NEARLY GOT TO YOU!
10

— OF COURSE, KEVIN... WELL, NO, I...

— WHAT?! YOU DON'T KNOW WHO THE FATHER IS?

I FOUND THIS TUNNEL A MONTH AGO...

— WHAT DOES IT MATTER? IT WILL BE YOU IF YOU SO WISH...

— FORGIVE ME, DAISY. MY HOUSE WILL BE YOURS!

...THERE WERE JUST A HANDFUL OF YARDS TO GO...

— THANK YOU, KEVIN. I WAS SURE I COULD COUNT ON YOU NOW THAT I'VE BEEN CUT OUT OF THE WILL...

— WHAT?!

...THE GUY WHO DUG IT MUST HAVE PREFERRED THE SOAP OVER HIS FREEDOM!

AN EASY JOB FOR SOMEONE WITH WILLPOWER!...

THE DIRECTOR WILL HAVE TO MAKE A CORRECTION...

...99.9% METHOD.

14

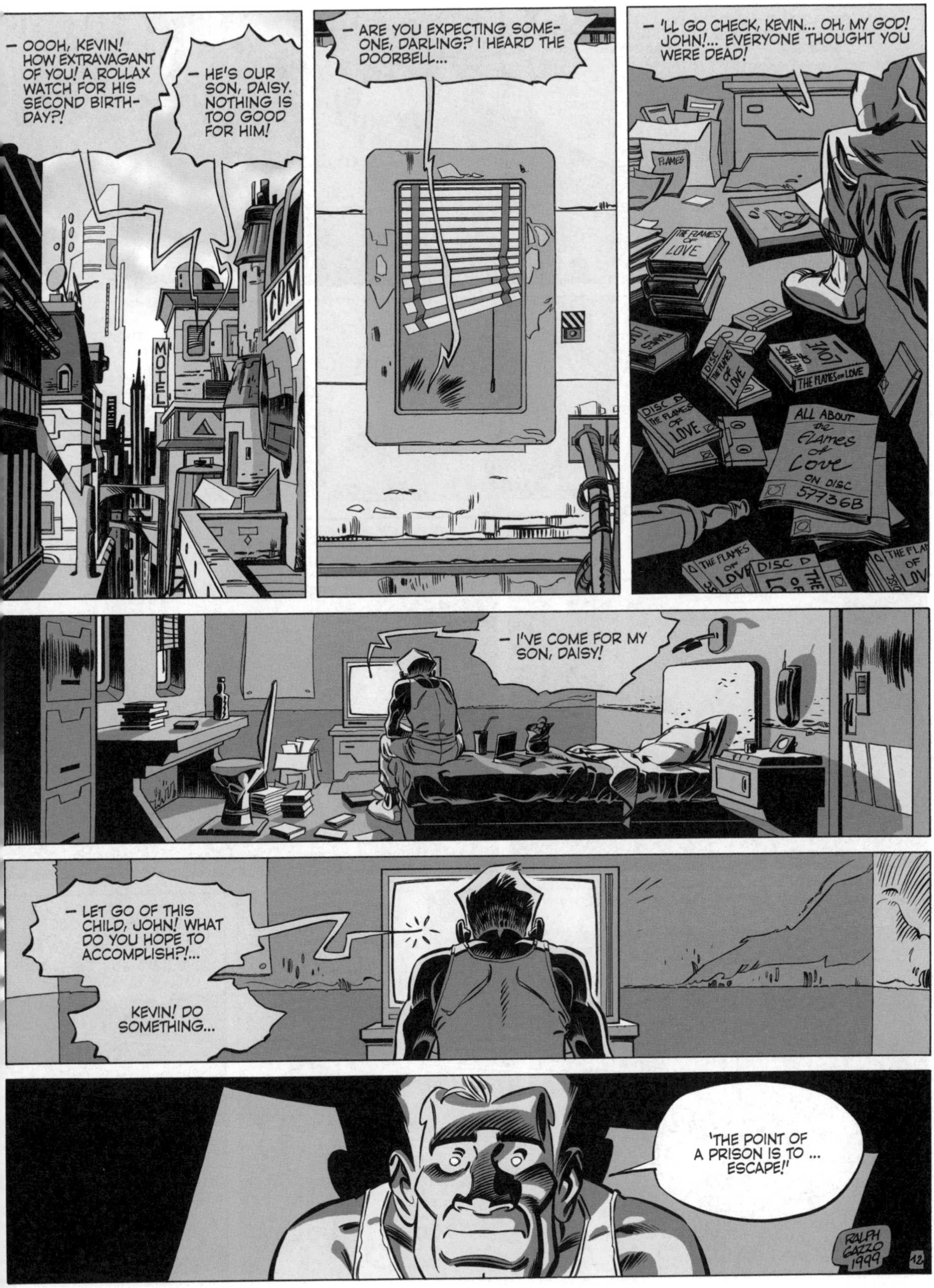
– OOOH, KEVIN! HOW EXTRAVAGANT OF YOU! A ROLLAX WATCH FOR HIS SECOND BIRTH-DAY?!
– HE'S OUR SON, DAISY. NOTHING IS TOO GOOD FOR HIM!
MOTEL
– ARE YOU EXPECTING SOME-ONE, DARLING? I HEARD THE DOORBELL...
– 'LL GO CHECK, KEVIN... OH, MY GOD! JOHN!... EVERYONE THOUGHT YOU WERE DEAD!
THE FLAMES OF LOVE
ALL ABOUT the Flames of Love ON DISC 57736B
– I'VE COME FOR MY SON, DAISY!
– LET GO OF THIS CHILD, JOHN! WHAT DO YOU HOPE TO ACCOMPLISH?!...
KEVIN! DO SOMETHING...
'THE POINT OF A PRISON IS TO ... ESCAPE!'
RALPH GAZZO 1999
12

I ALMOST DIDN'T READ IT, IT'S SO FULL OF SPELLING ERRORS.

BUT THE STYLE IS INTRIGUING: AUSTERE, JOURNALISTIC... I ALMOST FELT LIKE I WAS READING A NEWSPAPER ARTICLE FROM 2040. IT'S A WELCOME CHANGE FROM THE USUAL SCI-FI CLICHÉS.

IF I TOLD YOU THE STUFF I RECEIVE EVERY DAY!... ALIEN INVASIONS, INTERGALACTIC SUPERVILLAINS, GREEN MONSTERS...

SPEAKING OF MONSTER INVASIONS, I HAPPEN TO HAVE A...

?

ONE OF MY MAGAZINES COULD PUT OUT A SPECIAL SCIENCE-FICTION ISSUE ... BUT I'D NEED MORE MATERIAL.

TELL YOU WHAT: I'M WILLING TO PUBLISH THAT SHORT STORY IF YOU WRITE ME A SECOND ONE. HOW ABOUT IT?

AS MR WILSON'S LITERARY AGENT, I GLADLY ACCEPT THIS OFFER!

WHY DIDN'T YOU LET ME SHOW HIM MY MANUSCRIPT? THAT GUY LOVES MY WORK!

'YOUR' WORK?

WELL, I'M THE ONE WHO CAME UP WITH THE NAMES OF THE CHARACTERS IN THE FLAMES OF LOVE, AREN'T I?

ANYWAY... AS FOR YOUR MANUSCRIPT, I THINK IT'S BETTER TO WAIT A LITTLE LONGER. RIGHT NOW, LET'S GIVE THAT GUY THE SHORT STORY HE ASKED FOR.

OK, WELL... WHAT'LL IT BE ABOUT?

HOW SHOULD I KNOW? AREN'T YOU SUPPOSED TO BE THE MIS-UNDERSTOOD GENIUS HERE?!

I HAVE THE PERFECT TITLE!

MFF!

...TIP ...TAP...

HEY! I JUST GOT THIS IDEA ABOUT A MUTANT CROCODILE!

GAAAAH!

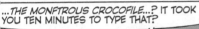

...THE MONSTROUS CROCOFILE...? IT TOOK YOU TEN MINUTES TO TYPE THAT?

IT'S THIS KEYBOARD — IT'S A CRAPPY LAYOUT!... I THINK SOMEONE SHOULD INVENT A SYSTEM THAT'D READ DIRECTLY FROM YOUR BRAIN!

I'LL DO THE TYPING, OK? IT'LL BE FASTER...

OH, YEAH? WELL, IN THAT CASE, WHY DON'T YOU DO EVERYTHING YOURSELF!?

AAARGH! THERE'S BACKFLOW FROM THE SEWERS AGAIN!

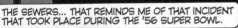

THE SEWERS... THAT REMINDS ME OF THAT INCIDENT THAT TOOK PLACE DURING THE '56 SUPER BOWL.

AS SOON AS I HAVE ENOUGH MONEY, I'M OUT OF THIS DUMP!

SO? DID YOU FIND A STORY?

COULD BE...

TIP...TAP...TAP...TIP...TAP...TIP...TAP...

...DON'T FORGET TO PUT A CROCODILE IN IT, OK?

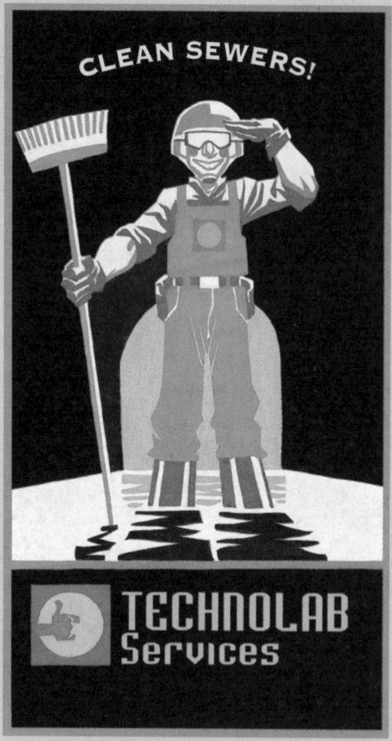
CLEAN SEWERS!
TECHNOLAB
Services

THE BIG FLUSH

MEGA YORK, 2067...

BAD NEWS, GUYS. I JUST RECEIVED A PRIORITY MISSION ORDER!

SEWER RANGERS

AN ELITE CORPS!
TECHNOLAB SERVICES

WE MUST RECOVER A KEY THAT AN EMPLOYEE OF THE DEPARTMENT OF DEFENCE ACCIDENTALLY DROPPED DOWN A SEWER GRATE. THE KEY GRANTS TOP-SECRET CLEARANCE, SO THIS IS A VITAL JOB.

WHICH GOES TO SHOW THAT WORKING AT THE DOD DOESN'T MEAN YOU AIN'T A DAMN FOOL!

KEEP YOUR COMMENTS TO YOURSELF, SANCHEZ. WE DON'T HAVE TIME TO WASTE!

BECAUSE TONIGHT'S THE SUPER BOWL*.

YEP! FIRST QUARTER'S ALMOST OVER!

THAT GIVES US ONLY 30-35 MINUTES BEFORE THE KEY'S CARRIED OFF BY THE BIG FLUSH!

BEEP

OK, PEOPLE, GET TO WORK!

THE BIG FLUSH! HAD TO HAPPEN TO US!

?

*FINAL GAME OF THE AMERICAN NATIONAL FOOTBALL LEAGUE ANNUAL CHAMPIONSHIP

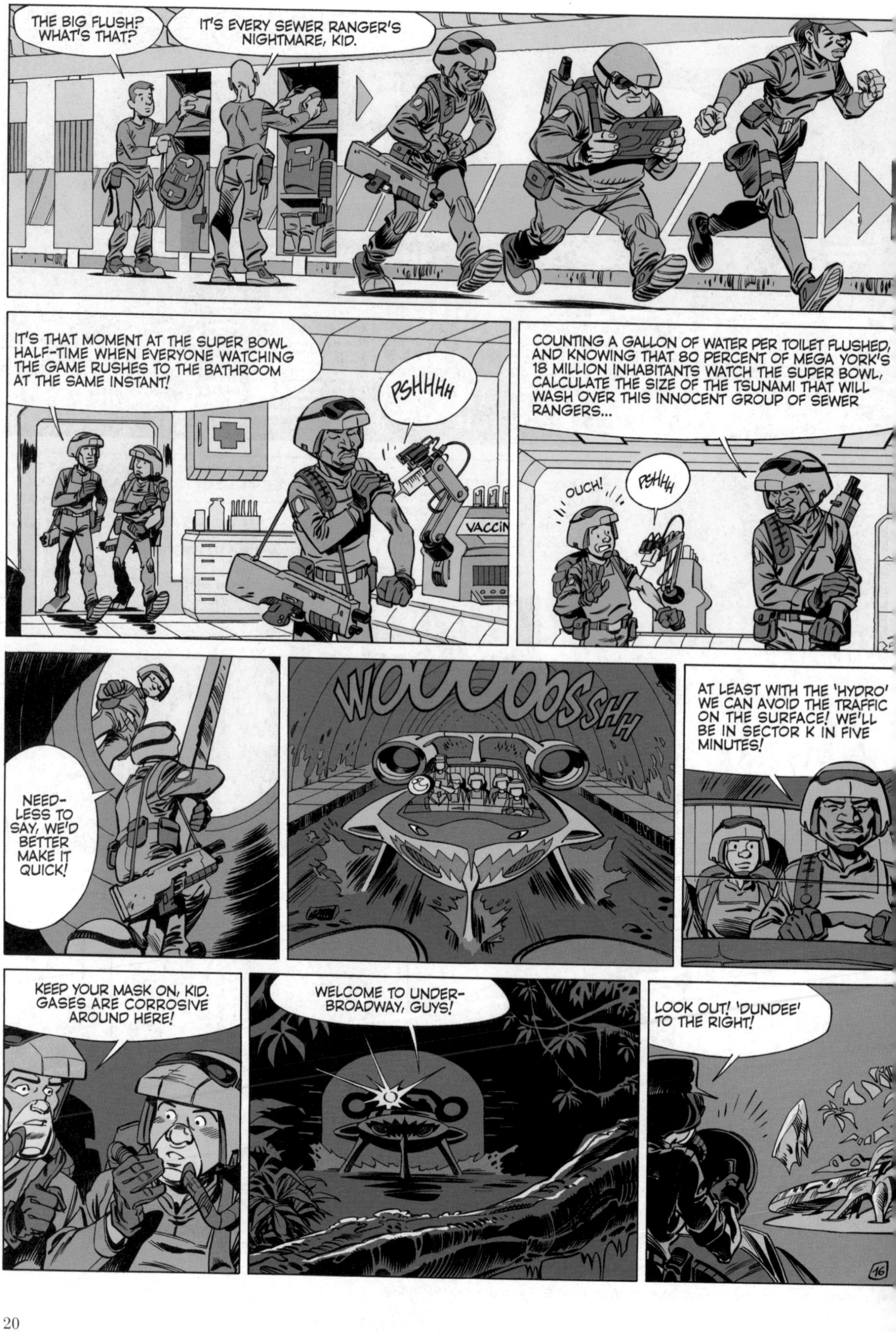
THE BIG FLUSH? WHAT'S THAT?
IT'S EVERY SEWER RANGER'S NIGHTMARE, KID.
IT'S THAT MOMENT AT THE SUPER BOWL HALF-TIME WHEN EVERYONE WATCHING THE GAME RUSHES TO THE BATHROOM AT THE SAME INSTANT!
PSHHHH
VACCIN
COUNTING A GALLON OF WATER PER TOILET FLUSHED, AND KNOWING THAT 80 PERCENT OF MEGA YORK'S 18 MILLION INHABITANTS WATCH THE SUPER BOWL, CALCULATE THE SIZE OF THE TSUNAMI THAT WILL WASH OVER THIS INNOCENT GROUP OF SEWER RANGERS...
OUCH!
PSHHH
NEED-LESS TO SAY, WE'D BETTER MAKE IT QUICK!
WOOOOOSSHH
AT LEAST WITH THE 'HYDRO' WE CAN AVOID THE TRAFFIC ON THE SURFACE! WE'LL BE IN SECTOR K IN FIVE MINUTES!
KEEP YOUR MASK ON, KID. GASES ARE CORROSIVE AROUND HERE!
WELCOME TO UNDER-BROADWAY, GUYS!
LOOK OUT! 'DUNDEE' TO THE RIGHT!
16

GROOAAArr

WHOA!

MY GOD! IT WAS ... MASSIVE!

THE CROCS AIN'T NOTHING. THEY'RE EASY TO SPOT!

NOT LIKE THE FLESH-EATING SQUIDS! NOW, THOSE ARE SNEAKY HOMBRES!

FLESH-EATING SQUIDS ?

IN THE 2020s, IT WAS VERY TRENDY TO KEEP ONE IN YOUR BATHTUB!

BUT AFTER PIRANHAS BECAME FASHIONABLE... SPLOOOOOSH! DOWN THE DRAIN WENT THE SQUIDS!

AND ONCE PIRANHAS WERE OUT, FLUSHHHH... MAKE WAY FOR TRANSGENIC MONGOOSES!

WE'RE HERE!

FIVE MINUTES LEFT ON THE CLOCK!

WE ONLY HAVE 15 MINUTES, THEN!

NOW THAT WE'VE AVOIDED THE TRAFFIC, WOULDN'T IT BE SAFER TO WALK UP TOP?

NEGATIVE. AFTER THE BIG FIRES OF '36, THE CITY WAS FORCED TO REBUILD IN A RUSH, ALL WILLY-NILLY. SINCE THEN, IT'S BEEN EASIER TO LOCATE A MAIN DRAIN THROUGH THE UNDERGROUND PASSAGES THAN FROM THE SURFACE.

BEEP BEEP

BEEP... BEEP... BEEP

TOXIC

BBRLLLB...

BEEP BEEP BEEP!

BLAADOFF

HOLY CRAP!

SBLEUUARBB

JEEZ! WHOEVER PISSED THIS HAD BETTER SEE A DOCTOR FAST!

MUST BE AN ILLEGAL INDUSTRIAL DISCHARGE! WE'LL NOTIFY THE ANTIPOLLUTION BRIGADE.

BLOF BLOF BLOF

BRLAOF...

WATCH WHERE YOU STEP!

DAMNED TOXIC WASTES...

THE BRONCOS JUST SCORED!

18

WWOOOSHHH

THE MAIN MUST BE JUST AHEAD!

WOOS

EEEEEEEKK

AAAAAH!

BRATATA

TATATATA

BRATATATATA

GO AWAY! GO AWAY!

TAT TATA

TATATATATATA

IT'S ALL RIGHT, KID. THEY'RE GONE.

WHAT WERE THOSE THINGS?

SOME SORT OF BABOONS, I RECKON...

DO BABOONS HAVE WEBBED FEET?

WE HAVE FIVE MINUTES LEFT, TOPS, GUYS.

YOU'RE UP, ROOKIE!

USUALLY, I WOULDN'T GIVE YOU SUCH AN IMPORTANT JOB SO SOON, BUT YOU WERE THE ONLY DIVER AVAILABLE TONIGHT. SORRY!

IT'S OK.

THE KEY WE'RE LOOKING FOR IS MADE OF TITANIUM. USE THIS DETECTOR.

THERE! A SIGNAL ...

...THEY MAKE TITANIUM SPOONS NOW?

ANOTHER SIGNAL!

YES!

WHAT'S HE DOING, DARN IT?

NO NEED TO WORRY. I'M SURE HE'S ALMOST DONE.

IT'S THE LAST PLAY

FLAODSH

HH... SORRY IT TOOK A WHILE... HH... BUT THERE WERE ... COMPLICATIONS... HH...

YEAH? WHAT KIND OF COMPLICA- TIONS?

THE VERY CLINGY KIND!

...COMMERCIALS HAVE STARTED!

SHHHFRRRFRHFRHHH

FRHHSHHH

HUNH!

FRSHRRHH

FLAOWOM

SHHHHHHHHH

WE'VE GOT THE KEY, BOSS. WHERE DO YOU WANT US TO BRING IT?

WHAT?

WHAT'S GOING ON?

WHAT'S GOING ON IS THAT I THINK OUR SUPERIORS TOOK US FOR A BUNCH OF DARNED FOOLS!

BLUB BLUB

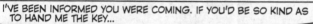

I'VE BEEN INFORMED YOU WERE COMING. IF YOU'D BE SO KIND AS TO HAND ME THE KEY...

MY FRIENDS AND I WOULD LIKE TO CLARIFY A CERTAIN POINT. YOU'VE GOT TWO SECONDS TO TELL ME WHO YOU WERE SUPPOSED TO GIVE THE KEY TO.

KLIK KLAK

I SEE PEOPLE COMING TO RETURN YOUR KEY, DAVE, JUST LIKE YOU SAID.

DIDN'T I TELL YOU? I NEED ONLY SNAP MY FINGERS TO GET EVERYTHING I WANT!

SO, THE SECRETARY'S PRECIOUS SON DROPPED THE KEYS TO HIS PORSCHE DOWN A SEWER GRATE?

I SUPPOSE CALLING A CAB TO GET HOME WOULD HAVE BEEN PHYSICALLY PAINFUL.

ER... WELL, YOU SEE...

WAIT. WHAT EXACTLY ARE YOU...?

SINCE YOU DON'T SEEM TO REALISE HOW DIFFICULT OUR JOB IS, WE'RE GOING TO GIVE YOU A QUICK GLIMPSE AT IT — FREE OF CHARGE!

THE EXIT'S 200 YARDS TO THE LEFT!

DON'T FORGET YOUR KEY!

PLOOSH

BY THE WAY, ISN'T THE NEAREST EXIT TOWARDS THE RIGHT?

YOU THINK SO? HUH. ANYONE CAN MAKE A MISTAKE!

EEEEEK!

AAAHHHHH!

I READ YOUR STORIES, WILSON.

THERE'S SOME GOOD STUFF IN THERE. BUT, HONESTLY, YOUR STYLE IS A DISASTER!

IF YOU ASKED ME HERE JUST TO INSULT ME, I'M LEAVING RIGHT NOW!

...WILSON, HAVE YOU EVER CONSIDERED BEING A WRITER FOR TV?... I WORK FOR A BIG NETWORK AND WE'RE LOOKING FOR FRESH TALENT...

WE'RE LAUNCHING A NEW SCI-FI ANTHOLOGY SERIES – KINDA LIKE *THE TWILIGHT ZONE.*

OH, RIGHT, YEAH! THAT SHOW WAS SO SPOOKY, WITH THAT THEME MUSIC: 'TADADADAH TADADADAH'.

WHOA! WORKING FOR TV! THAT'S SO AWESOME!

A SPOOKY SCI-FI TALE... LET'S SEE IF I CAN REMEMBER THAT STORY WE USED TO TELL EACH OTHER AS KIDS ON HALLOWEEN NIGHT...

WRITE ME AN EPISODE. IF WE LIKE IT, WE'LL TALK ABOUT WORKING TOGETHER.

YES... THAT WAS BACK WHEN TECHNOLAB WAS IN CHARGE OF THE SPACE 'LIGHTHOUSES'. THEY SERVED AS RELAY-BEACONS FOR REMOTE-CONTROLLED TRANSPORT BARGES OPERATING IN THE OUTER SOLAR SYSTEM.

TADADADAH... TADADADAAAH...

PROPER OPERATION OF SUCH BASES REQUIRED A HUMAN PRESENCE, BUT THE SOLITUDE THOSE MEN FACED WAS TERRIBLE... ALMOST UNBEARABLE.

HOW DID THAT STORY GO AGAIN?...

SPACE TO YOUR
MEASURE

TECHNOLAB Space

# THE DAY OF THE DEAD

'HALF ASLEEP I HEAR A VOICE, IS IT ONLY IN MY MIND?'... ♪

'OR IS IT SOMEONE CALLING ME?'... ♪ ♪

ONLY THIRTEEN DAYS TILL I'M RELIEVED... NOT A MINUTE TOO SOON!

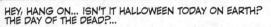

HEY, HANG ON... ISN'T IT HALLOWEEN TODAY ON EARTH? THE DAY OF THE DEAD?...

...'SOMEONE I FAILED AND LEFT BEHIND.' ♪

NOT THAT THERE'S ANY CHANCE OF TRICK-OR-TREATERS RINGING MY DOORBELL...

?

24

WHAT'S GOING ON HERE?

HOW COME NONE OF MY INSTRUMENTS DETECTED THAT SHIP? THAT'S JUST NOT POSSIBLE!

STATION TELES IV CALLING EARTH. I HAVE A SHIP ON APPROACH HERE. WHY DID NOBODY BOTHER TO INFORM ME, DARNIT?

SCRRSH... SCRRSH... SCRRSH... SCRRRHH... ...

EARTH? COME IN, EARTH...

NO NEED TO PANIC... THE AIRLOCK WON'T OPEN FROM THE OUTSIDE UNLESS I LET IT. THESE GUYS WILL HAVE TO CONTACT ME IF THEY WANT TO GET IN!

?!

NO...

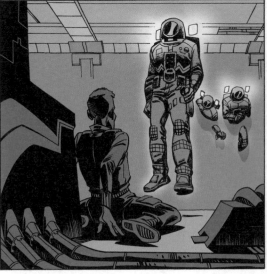

OH... OH, LORD, HAVE MERCY ON ME!

IT'S AS WE THOUGHT, CAPTAIN. WE'RE IN THE WRECK OF THE TELES IV.

THE WRECK OF...

THE MARS ORBITAL STATION THAT BLEW UP TEN YEARS AGO.

YEP. HAPPENED ON HALLOWEEN. THE GUY ON BOARD DIDN'T MAKE IT.

WHAT DID YOU SAY?!

LET'S GO, GUYS. NO POINT IN STAYING HERE.

THIS PLACE GIVES ME THE CREEPS.

LORD, HAVE MERCY ON ME...

WITH US TONIGHT IS MR WILSON, WHOSE SCRIPTS HAVE BEEN BREAKING AUDIENCE RECORDS ON OUR CHANNEL THESE LAST FEW MONTHS.

HELLO, YES?

YOUR STORIES OFFER A RATHER CHILLY VISION OF OUR FUTURE... WHERE DO YOU GET ALL YOUR IDEAS?

YES, YES, HE'S ON IT. HE'LL HAVE THE SCRIPT READY BY TOMORROW WITHOUT FAIL!

OH, IT'S EASY: I HAVE A GHOSTWRITER, LIKE EVERYONE ELSE!...

HA! HA!

...BUT, JOKING ASIDE, IT'S ALL ABOUT WORK. YOU HAVE TO KEEP PRODUCING MATERIAL, AND MORE MATERIAL. THAT'S THE KEY TO SUCCESS.

THE GALL OF THAT GUY...

WORST THING IS, HE'S RIGHT... I HAVE TO WRITE AND REWRITE, AGAIN AND AGAIN... NEVER STOP...

...HOLD ON, NO MATTER WHAT... 'CAUSE OF THE FUTURE OF MANKIND BEING IN THE BALANCE AND ALL THAT JAZZ...

RIGHT... BACK TO WORK...

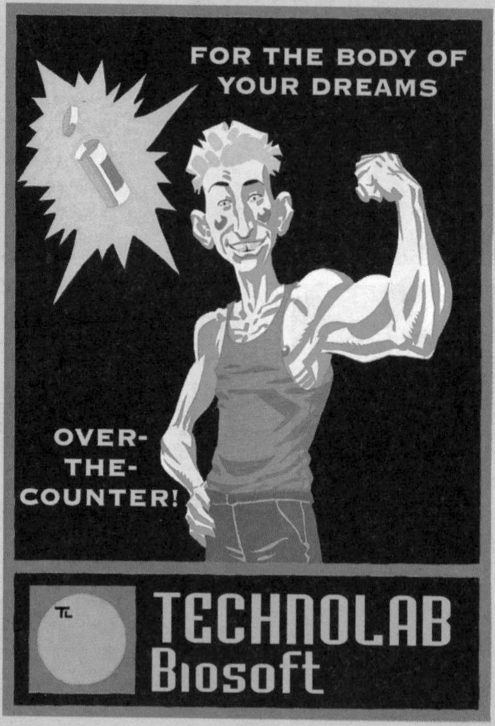
FOR THE BODY OF
YOUR DREAMS
OVER-
THE-
COUNTER!
TECHNOLAB
Biosoft

A HURRIED MAN

...WE'RE NOW SEEING THE HISTORIC VICTORY FOR *THROPERITHEIN©* AT THE BEIJING OLYMPICS OF 2023...

32 GOLD MEDALS... THE BIOSOFT TEAM — A SUBSIDIARY OF TECHNOLAB — COMPLETELY DOMINATED ITS COMPETITORS GENOTECH AND GENERAL LABORATORY.

HERE'S A WONDERFUL PERFORMANCE BY ... OH, DRAT, WHAT WAS THE NAME OF THAT SPRINTER AGAIN?... BRENDON? BENSON?

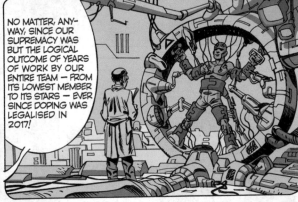

NO MATTER, ANYWAY, SINCE OUR SUPREMACY WAS BUT THE LOGICAL OUTCOME OF YEARS OF WORK BY OUR ENTIRE TEAM — FROM ITS LOWEST MEMBER TO ITS STARS — EVER SINCE DOPING WAS LEGALISED IN 2017!

A WONDERFUL HUMAN ADVENTURE THAT CONTINUES TO THIS DAY, AND WHOSE GOAL WILL ALWAYS BE TO HELP EXPAND THE LIMITS OF THE BODY.

YEAH, OK. I ALREADY KNOW ALL THAT.

OF COURSE, BUT THE CONTRACT YOU'RE ABOUT TO SIGN REQUIRES THAT WE PROPERLY REPRESENT OUR COMPANY.

THIS CONTRACT ALSO STIPU-LATES THAT YOU RENOUNCE ALL POSSIBLE LAWSUITS AGAINST OUR COMPANY FOR ANY SIDE EFFECTS OF THE PRODUCT YOU'RE GOING TO TEST FOR US.

LET'S PROCEED WITH THE INJECTION NOW.

HEY, LOOK. IF IT ISN'T SUPER GUINEA PIG!

WHOO! AND HE DRESSED TO THE NINES FOR IT!

HEY, GUYS!

SO, DID THE STUFF THEY PUMPED INTO YOU HURT

HOW D'YOU FEEL?

I FEEL LIKE A MILLION DOLLARS. COULD BE BECAUSE OF ALL THE MONEY IN MY POCKET, THOUGH!

HAHA!

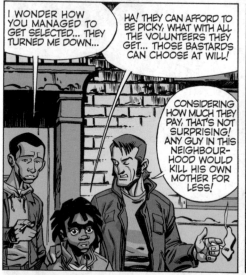

I WONDER HOW YOU MANAGED TO GET SELECTED... THEY TURNED ME DOWN...

HA! THEY CAN AFFORD TO BE PICKY, WHAT WITH ALL THE VOLUNTEERS THEY GET... THOSE BASTARDS CAN CHOOSE AT WILL!

CONSIDERING HOW MUCH THEY PAY, THAT'S NOT SURPRISING! ANY GUY IN THIS NEIGHBOURHOOD WOULD KILL HIS OWN MOTHER FOR LESS!

THING IS, THEY WANT PEOPLE IN SUPER SHAPE... AND I WAS THE BEST AT 400-METRE HURDLES IN HIGH SCHOOL!

A CHUBBY SLOB LIKE YOU? WHO'S GONNA BELIEVE THAT?!

A THOUSAND BUCKS I MAKE IT TO THE END OF THE STREET BEFORE YOU!

?! HEY!

JUST YOU WAIT!

General Laboratory®

HOLY CRAP!... YOU'RE JUST ... TOO ... FAST!...

HAHAHA!

TONIGHT, NO ONE CAN CATCH ME!

MA'AM? THERE'S A RATHER AGITATED GENTLEMAN ASKING TO SEE YOU.

AH, MR IBAN. YOU LOOK TIRED. DO TAKE A SEAT!

...I CAN'T... BECAUSE OF THAT PRODUCT YOU INJECTED ME WITH YESTERDAY...

I COULDN'T STOP MOVING ALL NIGHT... IT FEELS LIKE ELECTRIC SHOCKS THROUGHOUT MY BODY ANY TIME MY MUSCLES ARE AT REST. IT'S UNBEARABLE!

AND I'M ABSOLUTELY STARVING! IT HURTS!... MY BODY'S GONE MAD; IT... IT'S GONE INTO OVERDRIVE! YOU'VE GOT TO STOP IT!

PLEASE, CALM DOWN. WE'LL START BY TAKING A SAMPLE OF YOUR BLOOD; THEN WE CAN DETERMINE WHAT TO DO...

BUT I **CAN'T** WAIT! DON'T YOU UNDERSTAND? I CAN'T STAND IT ANY MORE!

DON'T GO! WE'LL TAKE CARE OF YOU!

THERE'S NOT ENOUGH ROOM HERE... I FEEL... I CAN'T BREATHE!

31

HEY! COME BACK, YOU ...

HOT DOG

OOF!

THIEF! SOMEONE STOP HIM!

!

!!

HEY!

GOOD LUCK STOPPING THAT GUY!

UNBELIEV-ABLE!

32

...I DON'T GIVE A DAMN ABOUT A 'SNAG'! FIND ME THAT MAN!

WELL?

HE'S STOLEN FOOD FROM ABOUT 30 DIFFERENT PLACES ALL DAY, BUT NO ONE'S MANAGED TO STOP HIM... HE'S UNBELIEVABLY FAST!

THIS WHOLE BUSINESS IS STARTING TO GIVE US BAD PRESS... HOW MUCH LONGER DO YOU THINK THAT MAN CAN KEEP GOING?

SOME OF OUR PROJECTIONS GIVE HIM ABOUT FIVE OR SIX HOURS BEFORE HE COLLAPSES... OTHERS GIVE HIM A WHOLE DAY...

YOU HAVE TO STOP HIM. NOW.

...YES, OF COURSE!

HE'S ON THE LINE! HE WANTS TO TALK TO YOU!

HELLO, MR IBAN? YOU MUST TELL US WHERE YOU ARE! WE'LL HELP YOU!

I'M IN THE MILLENIA TOWER. 'BORROWED' AN EMPLOYEE'S CELL PHONE TO CALL YOU.

YOU CAN STOP WORRYING ABOUT ME. YOUR DRUG WAS GOOD FOR ME IN THE END. IT OPENED UP NEW HORIZONS.

WHAT DO YOU MEAN?

I DON'T FEEL TIRED ANY MORE. I DON'T FEEL PAIN... I'M LIKE A GOD!

33

LIKE YOU, I BELIEVE THAT ... THE BODY'S LIMITS CAN BE PUSHED BACK...

...THAT THEY CAN BE PUSHED ALL THE WAY BACK...

...THAT THERE'S NOTHING I CAN'T DO NOW.

...WHAT ARE YOU TALKING ABOUT? PLEASE COME BACK TO THE LAB!

...I'LL CALL YOU BACK IN FIVE MINUTES.

THEY TOTALLY LOVED THAT LAST EPISODE OF OUR SERIES. YOU KNOW, THE ONE WITH THE DUDE WHO KEEPS RUNNING.

YES, I KNOW, THANKS.

THEY EVEN WANT TO MAKE IT INTO A MUSICAL — WITH BRUCE WILLIS! ISN'T THAT AWESOME?

WHAT A RIDICULOUS IDEA!

OH YEAH, AND I SIGNED A CONTRACT WITH TOYWORLD TO MAKE TOYS OF THE MAIN CHARACTER!

WHAT?... YOU'RE KIDDING?!

YOU MORON! THIS GOES COMPLETELY AGAINST THE SPIRIT OF MY STORY!

SQUEAK

WHAT'S GOT INTO YOU? I THOUGHT YOU WANTED TO HELP ME MAKE IT BIG!...

YES, YOU'RE RIGHT... I MUST BE TIRED...

HERE'S YOUR LATEST STORY. I... I HAVE TO GET BACK TO WORK.

AH, VERY GOOD.

BUT, YOU KNOW, I TRUST YOU COMPLETELY NOW. YOU CAN SEND IT DIRECTLY TO THE PRODUCERS!

35

The Judgement of Solomon

...LADIES AND GENTLEMEN, WE ARE ABOUT TO RETURN TO OUR LIVE COVERAGE OF THE OREN-BELNAS-TECHNOLAB TRIAL.

A QUICK RECAP FOR THOSE OF OUR VIEWERS WHO MIGHT HAVE SPENT THE LAST FEW YEARS ON MARS: JOSEPH OREN, A SEVEN-YEAR-OLD CHILD PRODIGY, INVENTED A WEB CODING PROCESS THAT COULD MAKE WHOEVER DEPLOYS IT 30 BILLION eDOLLARS.

HIS LEGAL MOTHER — 35, SINGLE — WAS ORIGINALLY SUPPOSED TO MANAGE HIS ASSETS UNTIL HE CAME OF AGE. BUT MRS BELNAS, WHO WAS JOSEPH'S BIRTH MOTHER, FILED FOR CUSTODY OF 'HER' CHILD.

MRS BELNAS CLAIMS THAT MRS OREN ONLY 'BOUGHT' JOSEPH ON A WHIM.

WE'RE LIVE IN SIX MINUTES. HURRY UP!

...THAT OREN WOMAN, SHE DIDN'T WANT HER BELLY STRETCHED BY NO PREGNANCY!... BUT I BROUGHT THAT CHILD INTO THE WORLD! AND THERE AIN'T A DAY GOES BY I DON'T THINK ABOUT HIM!

ISN'T YOUR BELATED REMORSE SOMEWHAT ... OPPORTUNISTIC?

...BACK THEN I DIDN'T HAVE NO MONEY. COULDN'T TAKE CARE OF HIM... BUT I'VE GOT A JOB NOW! I WANT MY SON BACK!

IN A DRAMATIC UPSET THREE MONTHS AGO, MRS BELNAS'S LAWYERS SUCCEEDED IN PROVING THAT MRS OREN SPENT A MERE THREE PERCENT OF HER TIME WITH THE CHILD.

IT THREW THE OREN TEAM INTO TURMOIL.

MY CLIENT IS VERY BUSY WITH HER WORK, BUT SHE'S ALWAYS PROVIDED JOSEPH WITH THE BEST OF EVERYTHING!

A CHILD'S AFFECTION CANNOT BE BOUGHT!

BUT THE BIGGEST SURPRISE CAME FROM BIOTECH COMPANY TECHNOLAB, WHICH HAD, AT MRS OREN'S REQUEST, DONE SOME GENETIC MODIFICATIONS ON THE CHILD BEFORE HIS BIRTH.

THERE, SWEETIE. YOU'RE VERY HANDSOME.

THE NEURONAL CONNECTIONS THAT ALLOWED JOSEPH TO COME UP WITH HIS INVENTION WERE THE DIRECT RESULT OF THE MANIPULATIONS OUR COMPANY PERFORMED ON HIS GENOME.

AS SUCH A GENETIC IMPROVEMENT FALLS UNDER A TECHNOLAB PATENT, WE'D BE WITHIN OUR RIGHTS TO DEMAND A SHARE OF THE PROFITS GENERATED BY JOSEPH'S WORK. BUT WE OPTED FOR A MORE FLEXIBLE APPROACH, MORE IN ACCORDANCE WITH OUR COMPANY'S SPIRIT.

AS A RESULT OF HIS EXTRAORDINARY IQ, WE'RE ASKING THAT THE CHILD BE CONSIDERED A LEGAL ADULT AND THEREFORE ABLE TO FREELY DECIDE ON A SOLUTION HE FINDS SUITABLE.

HE'S READY.

AT THAT POINT, WE'LL EXTEND THE FOLLOWING OFFER TO HIM: WORK FOR US, WITH A SALARY OF e$3,000,000 A YEAR, COMPLETE ACCESS TO ALL OUR FACILITIES AND EQUIPMENT, AND THE FOSTER FAMILY OF HIS CHOICE IN FLORIDA.

...A 'CHOICE' CONTESTED BY THE OREN AND BELMAS FAMILIES, WHO ARGUE THAT IT REPRESENTS 'UNACCEPTABLE PRESSURE' PUT ON A STILL-IMMATURE CHILD.

...OH! I'M BEING TOLD THAT RIOTS HAVE ERUPTED IN LONDON OVER THIS TRIAL.

YES, BOB! VIOLENT CLASHES ARE CURRENTLY TAKING PLACE BETWEEN THE 'PRO-BIO' AND THE 'PRO-CHOICE'!...

LET THE CHILD DECIDE FOR HIMSELF!

GIVE HIM BACK TO HIS BIOLOGICAL MOTHER!

...MOTHER NATURE'S SACRED RIGHTS!!!

...RESPECT THE CHILD!!

37

ONE MINUTE TO LIVE FEED!

MR VALARD, IN YOUR BOOK YOU COMPARE THIS TRIAL TO THE JUDGEMENT OF SOLOMON. CAN YOU EXPLAIN THAT FOR OUR 150 MILLION VIEWERS?

ER... WELL, IN THE BIBLE, SOLOMON MUST CHOOSE BETWEEN TWO WOMEN WHO FIGHT OVER THE SAME CHILD.

...BUT WITH THE NUMBER OF PLAINTIFFS TODAY, THE OREN CASE IS RATHER MORE COMPLEX...

YOU'D HAVE TO CHOP THAT CHILD INTO THREE OR FOUR PIECES!... OK, THEY'RE TELLING ME THAT THE TRIAL IS ABOUT TO CONTINUE!

POOR KID...

EXIT

HE CUTS THE DISPUTE SHORT — IF YOU'LL PARDON THE PUN, HEH HEH — BY OFFERING TO CUT THE CHILD IN TWO. HE KNEW THAT THE REAL MOTHER WOULD BE THE ONE WHO'D REFUSE THAT JUDGEMENT, AND WHO'D GIVE HER CHILD UP RATHER THAN SEE HIM DIE...

IT'S THE MEDIA'S FAULT! VALARD

LET US RESUME THESE PROCEEDINGS.

TODAY'S HEARING WILL DETERMINE...

?

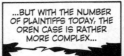

LOOK AT THE KID!

D'YOU THINK HE'S GOING TO SAY SOMETHING?

THAT'D BE A FIRST, FOR SURE!

36

THIS IS SECURITY. IT'S A HOMEMADE 'SPIDER' BOMB. NASTY THINGS — YOU CAN FIND THE BLUEPRINTS ONLINE... KEEP HIM BUSY; WE'RE EVACUATING THE BUILDING.

LISTEN, JOSEPH, YOU...

CLICK!

00.00.20

00.00.19  00.00.18

EXIT

EEEEEEEAAAA!!

EXIT

39

OUT OF MY WAY!

SHE'S TRYING TO REMOVE THE BELT!

WHERE DID THAT CHICK COME FROM?

ONLY FIVE SECONDS LEFT!

EEEEEEEEEEEE!!!

SCRsssshhhh...

COUGH COUGH...

YOU'LL BE ALL RIGHT... IT'S ALL OVER.

...MOMMY?

YES, COME IN!

NOLAN... IT'S TERRIBLE!...

WHAT'S GOING ON?

THE BASTARDS!... THEY DUPED ME! I LOST EVERYTHING!

WHAT?

AFTER MY TRIP TO MONACO, I WENT TO OUR PRODUCERS TO ASK FOR A... A SMALL ADVANCE...

I DIDN'T READ CAREFULLY WHEN I SIGNED... ALL THE LICENSING RIGHTS TO MY STORIES BELONG TO THEM! WE'RE BROKE!

FOR CRYING OUT LOUD... THAT WAS ALL YOU HAD TO DO: TAKE CARE OF THE CONTRACTS! AND YOU EVEN SCREWED THAT UP!!!

BUT WE CAN STILL ... START OVER, WITH ANOTHER PRODUCER, RIGHT?...

I'M... I'M GOING TO...

SCRATCHHH

GNNNNN...

WHAT DO YOU THINK?

41

YOU WON'T SAY ANYTHING? YOU DON'T WANT TO WORK WITH ME ANY MORE, IS THAT IT?

IF I CAN'T EVEN COUNT ON MY FRIENDS, I MIGHT AS WELL GIVE IT ALL UP, THEN!

...I'VE HEARD THERE'S A SMALL COMPANY RECRUITING RIGHT NOW... TECHNOLAB, OR SOMETHING LIKE THAT...

MAYBE THEY'LL APPRECIATE ME FOR WHAT I'M REALLY WORTH...

SKRIIIIIITCH

GRNNNNN

...SO, IT SEEMS THAT THE PAST HAS A HIGH RESILIENCE... HISTORY TENDS TO REMAIN THE SAME, NO MATTER WHAT MODIFICATIONS YOU MAKE.

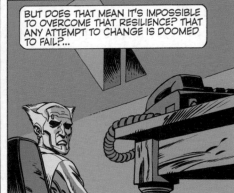

BUT DOES THAT MEAN IT'S IMPOSSIBLE TO OVERCOME THAT RESILIENCE? THAT ANY ATTEMPT TO CHANGE IS DOOMED TO FAIL?...

MAYBE YOU JUST NEED TO DISPLAY EXTRAORDINARY DETERMINATION.

HELLO, WILSON?... YEAH, IT'S ME. I THOUGHT ABOUT IT...

...I'LL GET BACK TO WORK.

49

EVER
STRONGER!

G TECHNOLAB Games

NIGHT OF THE SAMURAI

...HOT DIGGITY! I CAN'T BELIEVE WE DID IT! IT'S THE HEIST OF THE CENTURY, DUDE!

GOTTA HAVE AMBITION...

WE'RE RICH, SAMURAI! YOUR IDEA WAS PURE GENIUS!

WE CAN PAT OUR-SELVES ON THE BACK ONCE WE'VE DELIVERED THE 'ITEM' TO OUR CLIENT.

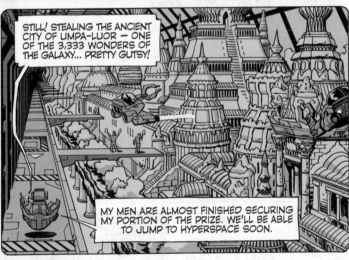

STILL! STEALING THE ANCIENT CITY OF UMPA-LUOR — ONE OF THE 3,333 WONDERS OF THE GALAXY... PRETTY GUTSY!

MY MEN ARE ALMOST FINISHED SECURING MY PORTION OF THE PRIZE. WE'LL BE ABLE TO JUMP TO HYPERSPACE SOON.

WHEN I TELL MY BUDDIES THAT...

SORRY TO INTERRUPT, GUYS, BUT I'VE GOT BAD NEWS...

A SWARM OF MARAUDER PIRATES JUST APPEARED IN SECTOR 5-34-12. LOOKS LIKE AN AMBUSH TO ME!

WHAT?

WARNING TO NEIGHBOUR-HOOD RESIDENTS: CITY UTILITIES WILL SHUT DOWN POWER IN FIVE MINUTES.

HUH?

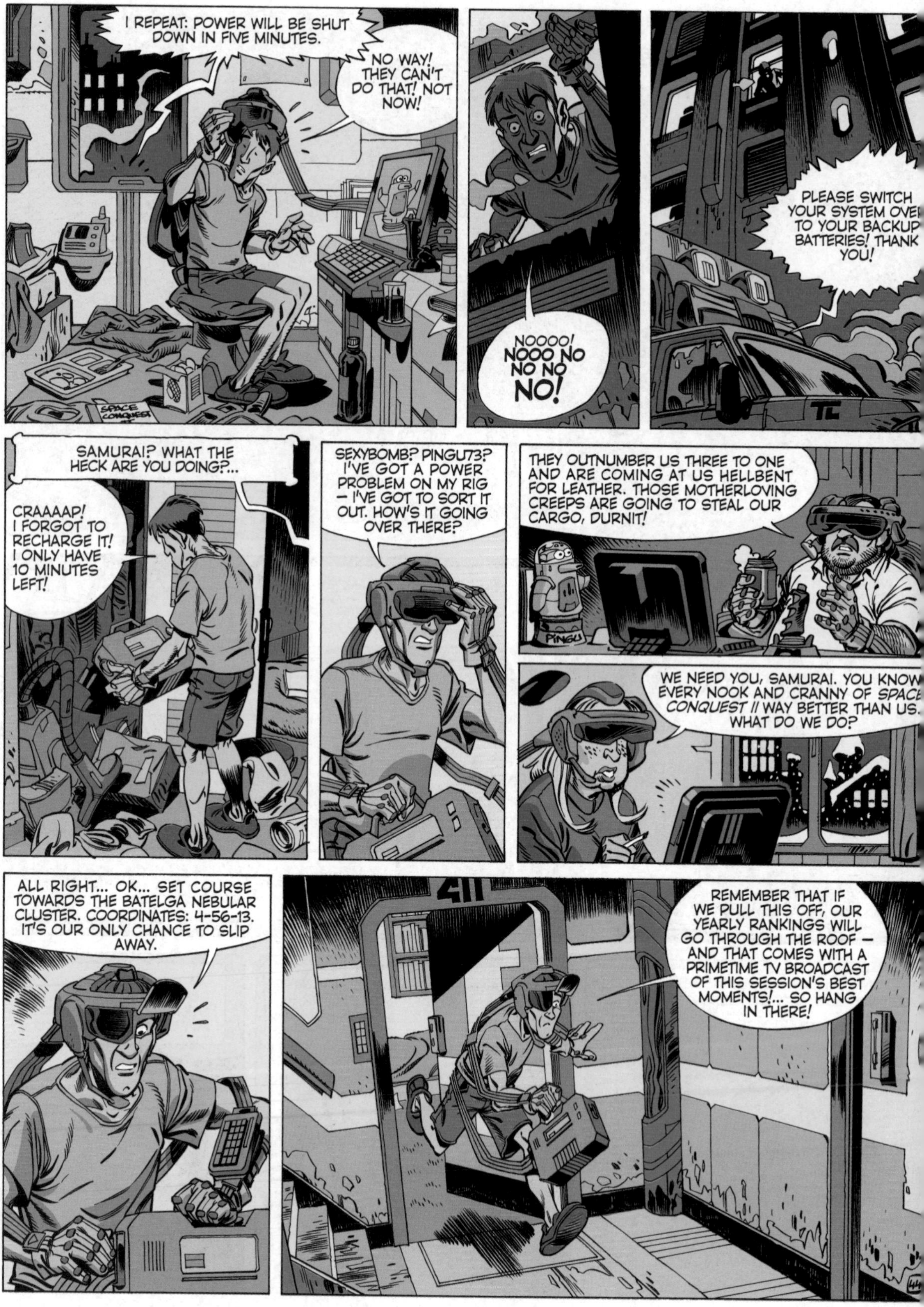
I REPEAT: POWER WILL BE SHUT DOWN IN FIVE MINUTES.
NO WAY! THEY CAN'T DO THAT! NOT NOW!
SPACE CONQUEST
NOOOO! NOOO NO NO NO NO!
PLEASE SWITCH YOUR SYSTEM OVE TO YOUR BACKUP BATTERIES! THANK YOU!
TC
SAMURAI? WHAT THE HECK ARE YOU DOING?...
CRAAAAP! I FORGOT TO RECHARGE IT! I ONLY HAVE 10 MINUTES LEFT!
SEXYBOMB? PINGU73? I'VE GOT A POWER PROBLEM ON MY RIG – I'VE GOT TO SORT IT OUT. HOW'S IT GOING OVER THERE?
THEY OUTNUMBER US THREE TO ONE AND ARE COMING AT US HELLBENT FOR LEATHER. THOSE MOTHERLOVING CREEPS ARE GOING TO STEAL OUR CARGO, DURNIT!
PINGU
WE NEED YOU, SAMURAI. YOU KNOW EVERY NOOK AND CRANNY OF SPACE CONQUEST II WAY BETTER THAN US. WHAT DO WE DO?
ALL RIGHT... OK... SET COURSE TOWARDS THE BATELGA NEBULAR CLUSTER. COORDINATES: 4-56-13. IT'S OUR ONLY CHANCE TO SLIP AWAY.
411
REMEMBER THAT IF WE PULL THIS OFF, OUR YEARLY RANKINGS WILL GO THROUGH THE ROOF – AND THAT COMES WITH A PRIMETIME TV BROADCAST OF THIS SESSION'S BEST MOMENTS!... SO HANG IN THERE!

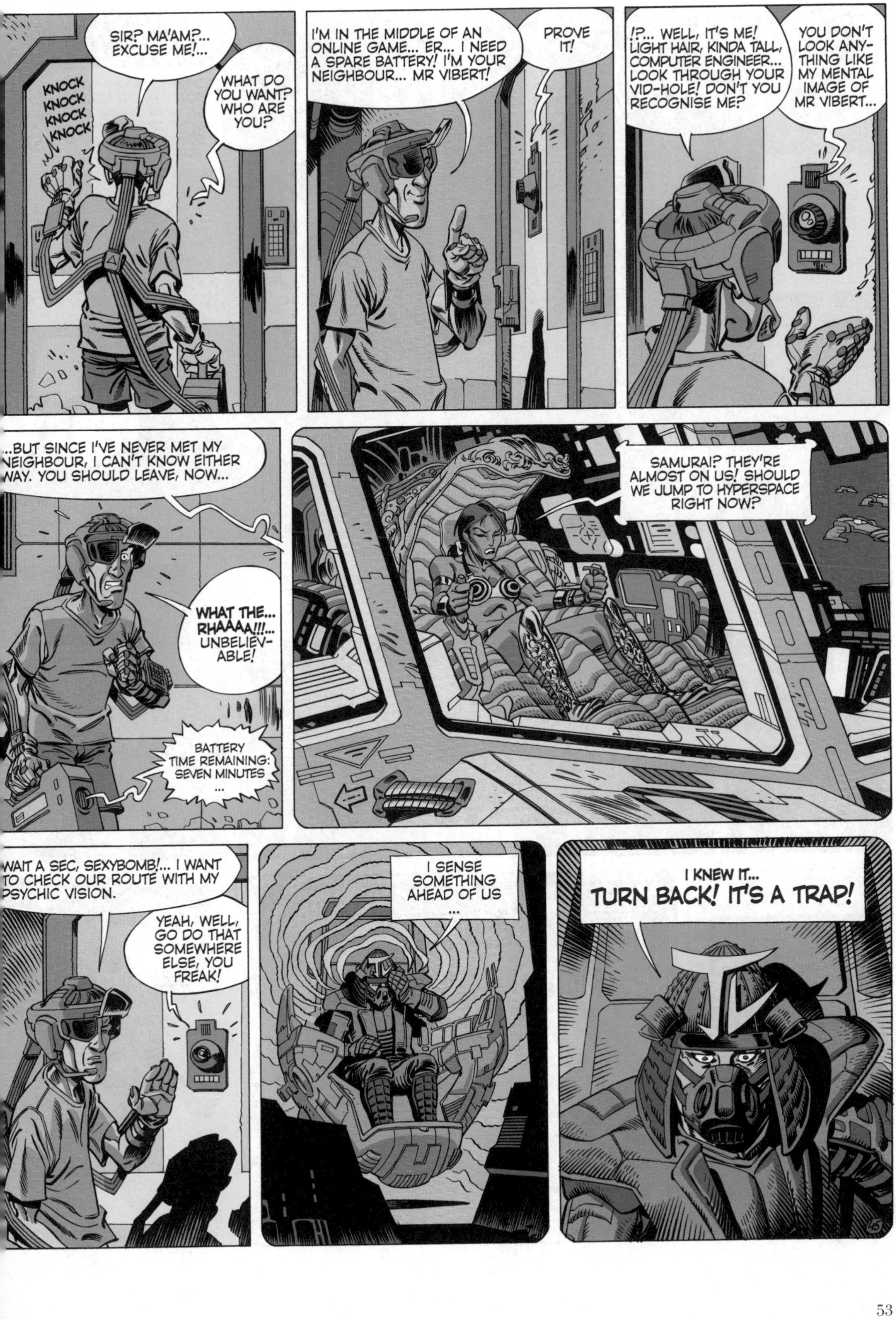
SIR? MA'AM?... EXCUSE ME!...
KNOCK KNOCK KNOCK KNOCK
WHAT DO YOU WANT? WHO ARE YOU?
I'M IN THE MIDDLE OF AN ONLINE GAME... ER... I NEED A SPARE BATTERY! I'M YOUR NEIGHBOUR... MR VIBERT!
PROVE IT!
!?... WELL, IT'S ME! LIGHT HAIR, KINDA TALL, COMPUTER ENGINEER... LOOK THROUGH YOUR VID-HOLE! DON'T YOU RECOGNISE ME?
YOU DON'T LOOK ANYTHING LIKE MY MENTAL IMAGE OF MR VIBERT...
...BUT SINCE I'VE NEVER MET MY NEIGHBOUR, I CAN'T KNOW EITHER WAY. YOU SHOULD LEAVE, NOW...
WHAT THE... RHAAAA!!!... UNBELIEVABLE!
BATTERY TIME REMAINING: SEVEN MINUTES ...
SAMURAI? THEY'RE ALMOST ON US! SHOULD WE JUMP TO HYPERSPACE RIGHT NOW?
WAIT A SEC, SEXYBOMB!... I WANT TO CHECK OUR ROUTE WITH MY PSYCHIC VISION.
YEAH, WELL, GO DO THAT SOMEWHERE ELSE, YOU FREAK!
I SENSE SOMETHING AHEAD OF US ...
I KNEW IT... TURN BACK! IT'S A TRAP!

WHAT'S HAPPENING? SOME OF MY SHIPS HAVE GONE CRAZY! THEY'RE THROWING THEMSELVES AT EACH OTHER!

TOTEMIC MINES. THEY DON'T SHOW UP ON THE STAR SONAR AND DISRUPT THE PSY-CONNECTIONS OF A SHIP'S COMPUTER.

I'M GOING TO CONTACT OUR OPPONENT... I WOULDN'T BE SURPRISED IF WE WERE UP AGAINST DARK VOODOO...

THE DARK VOODOO? THAT CANADIAN GUY WHO WAS ON THE COVER OF THE LATEST PADDLE MAG?

WE'RE TOAST, SEXYBOMB!... WE. ARE. TOAST. IT'S NOT FAIR!

GREETINGS, SAMURAI! HOW NICE TO FINALLY MEET. I'VE HEARD A LOT ABOUT YOU!

I'M FLATTERED...

NO, REALLY. YOU SEEM TO BE A PASSABLE PLAYER. I'M ALMOST SORRY THAT I HAVE TO SPACE-PAWN YOU.

BATTERY TIME REMAINING: FIVE MINUTES ...

WELL, I'D LOVE TO STAY AND CHAT, BUT I'VE GOT WORK TO DO: I NEED TO STEAL EVERYTHING YOU'RE TRANSPORTING AND ROCKET TO THE TOP OF SPACE CONQUEST II'S RANKINGS. HA HA HA!!...

BUH-BYE! – CLICK –

A PASSABLE PLAYER! THAT JERK!...

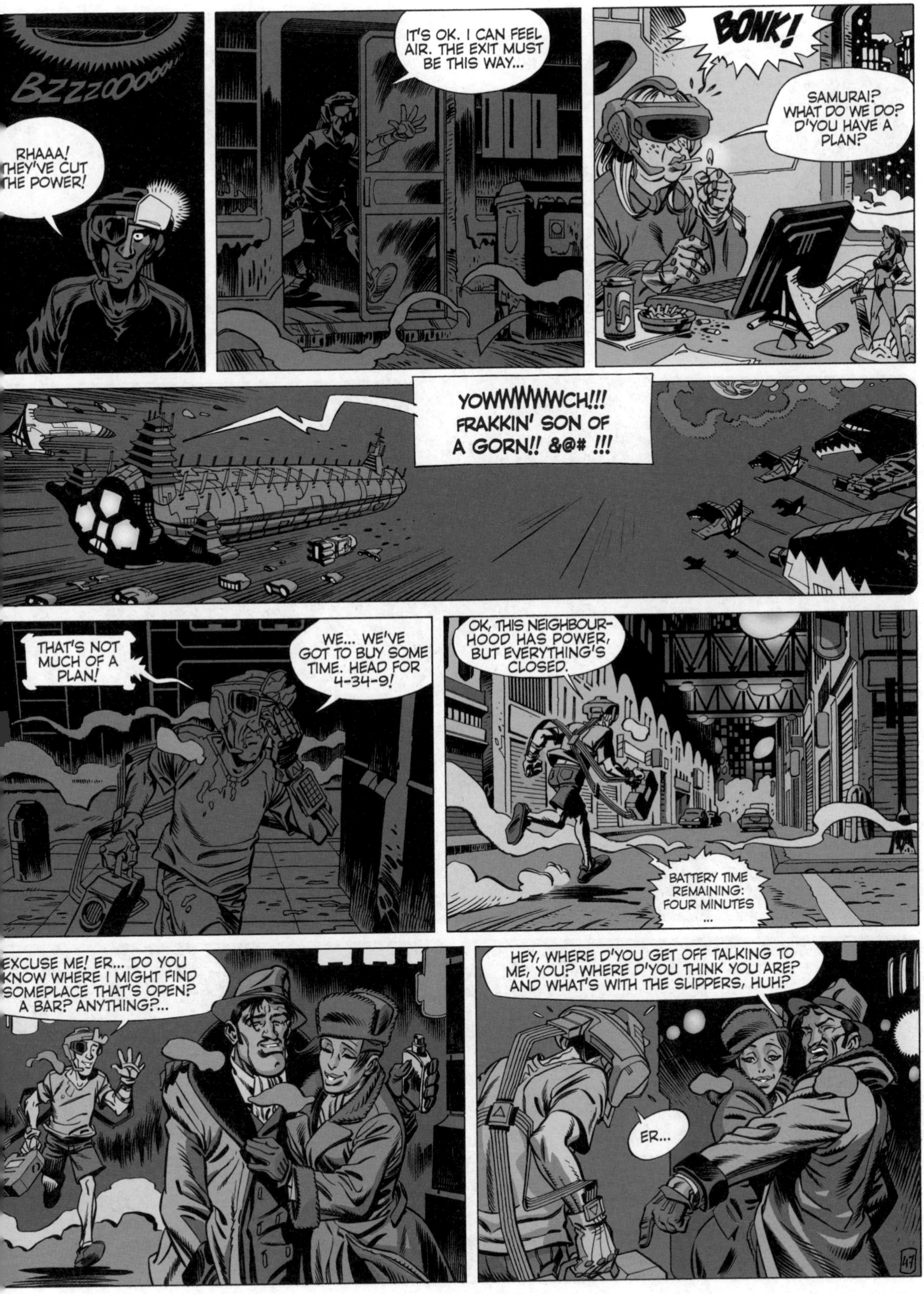
BZZZOOOOOH
RHAAA! THEY'VE CUT THE POWER!
IT'S OK. I CAN FEEL AIR. THE EXIT MUST BE THIS WAY...
BONK!
SAMURAI? WHAT DO WE DO? D'YOU HAVE A PLAN?
YOWWWWWCH!!! FRAKKIN' SON OF A GORN!! &@# !!!
THAT'S NOT MUCH OF A PLAN!
WE... WE'VE GOT TO BUY SOME TIME. HEAD FOR 4-34-9!
OK, THIS NEIGHBOURHOOD HAS POWER, BUT EVERYTHING'S CLOSED.
BATTERY TIME REMAINING: FOUR MINUTES ...
EXCUSE ME! ER... DO YOU KNOW WHERE I MIGHT FIND SOMEPLACE THAT'S OPEN? A BAR? ANYTHING?...
HEY, WHERE D'YOU GET OFF TALKING TO ME, YOU? WHERE D'YOU THINK YOU ARE? AND WHAT'S WITH THE SLIPPERS, HUH?
ER...
47

I'LL ... BE MOVING ON, THEN... THANKS!...

DON'T YOU RUN AWAY, LOSER! I AIN'T DONE TALKING TO YOU!

CRAAAAP... I HAVE NO IDEA WHERE TO GO! THIS SUCKS!

HOW ARE YOU DOING, GUYS

THEY'VE CAUGHT UP TO US!

...FOR REAL, DUDE, I DON'T SEE HOW WE CAN MAKE IT OUT OF THIS...

HE'S BROUGHT SOME MOREE-TITANS AS ALLIES...

ROOOOAAAA

56

WE DON'T STAND A CHANCE! LET'S JETTISON THE CARGO AND RUN WHILE WE STILL CAN...

WE HAVE ONE LAST CARD TO PLAY!

TWO YEARS AGO, I BOUGHT A CLASS IV PLASMA MISSILE!

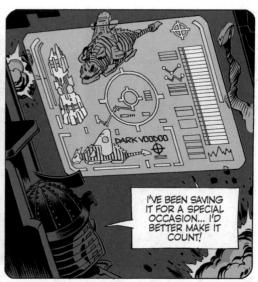

DARK VOODOO

I'VE BEEN SAVING IT FOR A SPECIAL OCCASION... I'D BETTER MAKE IT COUNT!

BATTERY TIME REMAINING: ONE MINUTE ...

CRAAAAAP! I NEED MORE TIME TO FIND A FIRING SOLUTION!

THERE! A GAS STATION! GIMME A SEC TO PLUG IN AND I'LL SHOOT DOWN VOODOO'S COMMAND SHIP...

OK, SAMURAI, BUT HURRY! THE MOREE-THINGIES ARE EATING US ALIVE!...

OUT FOR A WALK, ARE WE?

HOW ABOUT YOU COME WITH US INSTEAD?

LET ME GO!

BATTERY TIME REMAINING: 30 SECONDS...

WE'RE OUT OF TIME, SAMURAI...

I...

49

CUT IT OUT!...

I CALLED THE POLICE FROM MY COMPUTER!

OUTTA MY WAY, YOU RAT!

SPAK

YOU OK?

TO TELL YOU THE TRUTH, I FEEL KINDA CRAPPY...

THANK YOU SO MUCH! I DON'T KNOW WHAT WOULD HAVE HAPPENED IF YOU HADN'T COME ALONG!

THERE'S A GAS STATION THERE. BUY YOU COFFEE?

MESSAGE FROM PINGU73 TO SAMURAI: WHEN WE DIDN'T HEAR FROM YOU, WE CHOSE TO ABANDON THE CARGO AND SCRAM.

SORRY. I KNOW HOW IMPORTANT THIS MISSION WAS TO YOU...

BUT HEY... IT'S JUST A GAME, RIGHT? TTYL.

WILSON, SIGN UP WITH US?

IT'S WORTH CONSIDERING... MY PRODUCTION COMPANY IS YOUNG. WE'RE ALWAYS LOOKING FOR GOOD WRITERS!

THAT'S WHAT I THOUGHT.

THAT SAID, TO BE HONEST WITH YOU, WILSON BURNED A LOT OF BRIDGES IN THE BUSINESS... NO ONE SHED A TEAR OVER HIS FINANCIAL PROBLEMS!

I'VE NEVER MET SUCH A JACKASS SO PROUD OF BEING ONE ... AND I WORK FOR TV!

LISTEN... READ HIS LATEST SCRIPT ANYWAY.

WE'RE WILLING TO LET YOU HAVE IT FOR ... A VERY ADVANTAGEOUS PRICE...

OK, I'LL SEE WHAT I CAN DO.

YOU'RE A COMPLETE MYSTERY, NOLAN SKA... I'D LIKE TO KNOW WHAT A MAN OF YOUR CLASS IS DOING WITH WILSON.

THAT PARTICULAR STORY WOULD TAKE TOO LONG TO TELL...

51

THEY AGREED TO READ YOUR LATEST STORY.

HAHA! WE'RE BACK IN BUSINESS!

BUT I THINK WE NEED TO PUT PRESSURE ON THEM... MAKE THEM UNDERSTAND THAT THE GREAT WILSON IS BACK! LET'S DOUBLE OUR PRICES!

THAT WOULD BE A BAD IDEA...

I DON'T CARE WHAT YOU THINK! THIS IS ABOUT MY REPUTATION! I WANT THEM TO BEG ME TO COME BACK — ON THEIR KNEES!

YOUR REPUTATION? DO YOU REALLY WANT TO HEAR WHAT YOUR REPUTATION IS?

YEAH? YEAH? GO AHEAD!

A TERMINALLY ARROGANT TWERP WHO CONSTANTLY ACTS LIKE AN INSUFFERABLE BRAT!!!

IN SHORT, LOTS OF PEOPLE THINK YOU'RE A COMPLETE MORON!

OH, YEAH? WELL, THEN, WHY ARE YOU STILL WORKING WITH ME, HUH? HUH?

A LOT OF PEOPLE HAVE BEEN ASKING ME THAT VERY QUESTION LATELY!

LET ME TELL YOU WHY: BECAUSE YOU CAN'T DO WITHOUT ME! EVEN A COMPLETE MORON FIGURES IT OUT EVENTUALLY!

ARE YOU A BIT OF A PERV? OR MAYBE YOU FEEL LIKE I'M THE SON YOU NEVER HAD OR SOME CRAP LIKE THAT? WHO KNOWS!?

WHAT'S FOR SURE IS THAT I DO WHAT I WANT WITH YOU! 'CAUSE IF YOU HAD A LICK OF COMMON SENSE, YOU'D HAVE LEFT A LONG TIME AGO!

I'VE GOT YOU WRAPPED AROUND MY FINGER, YOU OLD FART! YOU'RE MINE!

SO YOU'RE GOING TO CALL THAT PRODUCER AND TELL HIM I WON'T SIGN FOR LESS THAN DOUBLE THE USUAL PRICE!

NEED TO CLEAR MY HEAD...

I DON'T KNOW IF I'LL HAVE THE STRENGTH TO KEEP AT IT FOR LONG...

53

THE TV SERIES IS DOING GREAT... BUT I'D LIKE TO REPUBLISH SOME OF YOUR SCRIPTS AS AN ANTHOLOGY.

IT DIDN'T TAKE ISABELLE LONG TO BELIEVE ME WHEN I TOLD HER I WAS WILSON'S GHOSTWRITER. SHE'S A SMART WOMAN.

WE COULD CALL IT *CLEAR BLUE TOMORROWS.* WHAT DO YOU THINK?

I OWE HER MY OWN SUDDEN SUCCESS, TOO.

GREAT IDEA!

OH, BY THE WAY: WILSON TRIED TO CONTACT YOU AGAIN. HE SAID HE WAS SORRY AND THAT HE WANTED TO WORK WITH YOU AGAIN.

WELL, YOU'LL HAVE TO TELL HIM TO GO TO HELL. AGAIN.

IS HE STILL WORKING AS A SALES REPRESENTATIVE FOR TECHNOLAB?

LAST I HEARD, HE WAS, YES.

IN ANOTHER LIFE, HE'D STARTED OUT AS A COURIER... WHO KNOWS? MAYBE I'VE MANAGED TO CHANGE HISTORY ENOUGH THAT IT'LL TAKE A DIFFERENT COURSE?

OR MAYBE WILSON WILL BECOME TECHNOLAB'S CEO ANYWAY?

I DON'T CARE ANY MORE!

HUMANITY WILL GET NO MORE THAN IT DESERVES...

F. VEHLMANN _ B. GAZZOTTI _ RALPH M

**TECHNOLAB Publishing**

WE THANK YOU FOR
READING ONE OF OUR
GRAPHIC NOVELS, AND
HOPE YOU ENJOYED IT.

ORDER YOUR NEW CATALOGUE NOW!

### RALPH MEYER
Artist

**B**orn in 1971, he dedicated himself from an early age to the joys of art, cloistered in a mysterious Buddhist monastery in south-south-east Tibet. Upon returning home, he drew the series *Berceuse Assassine* (his most important work, written by Tome). A fan of science fiction, he initiated the *Clear Blue Tomorrows* project, for which he recruited Bruno Gazzotti (who would draw all the right-hand panels) and Fabien Vehlmann (who handled the script).

### BRUNO GAZZOTTI
Artist

**B**orn in 1970, he dedicated himself from an early age to the joys of art, cloistered in a mysterious Buddhist monastery in south Tibet. Upon returning home, he drew the series *Soda* (his most important work, written by Tome – who's always putting his foot in it). A fan of science fiction, he initiated the *Clear Blue Tomorrows* project, for which he recruited Ralph Meyer (who would draw all the left-hand panels) and Fabien Vehlmann (who handled the script). He then returned to Tibet to create *Alone* (his new most important work, written by Fabien Vehlmann).

### FABIEN VEHLMANN
Writer

**B**orn in 1972, he dedicated himself from an early age to the joys of art, cloistered in a moderately mysterious Buddhist monastery in the south of Meuse. Upon returning home, he wrote the series *Green Manor* (his most important work, illustrated by Denis Bodard). A fan of science fiction, he wrote the *Clear Blue Tomorrows* project in a single night, then recruited Ralph Meyer and Bruno Gazzotti to draw just about every panel.